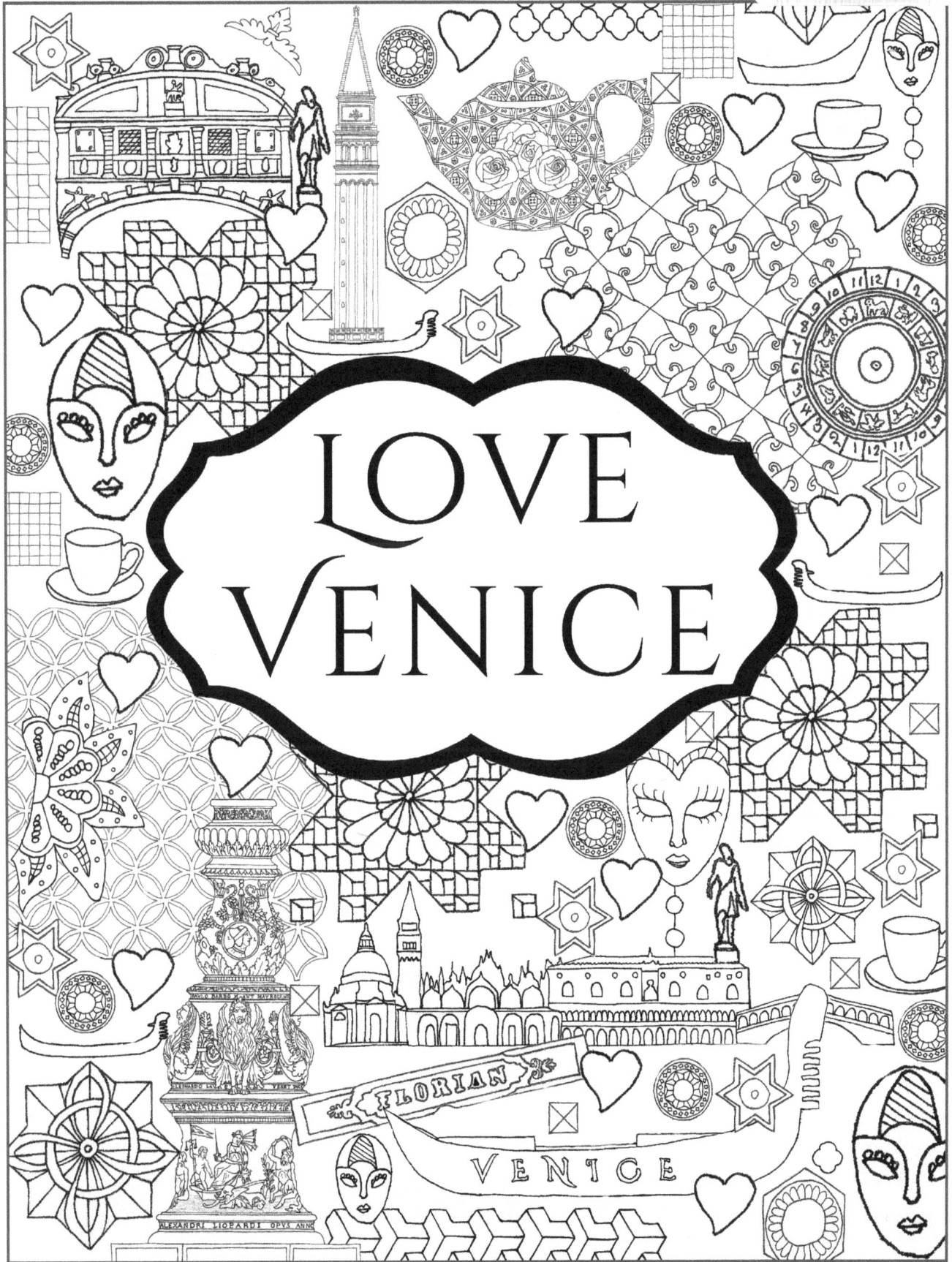

LOVE VENICE

FLORIAN

VENICE

Love Venice Adult Coloring Book for Mindfulness

First published in Great Britain in 2017 by Elmsbury Publishing UK

Copyright © 2017 Elmsbury Publishing UK

ISBN 978-0-9574878-57

www.elmsbury.com

ELMSBURY

Venice, the City of Water,

offers incredible inspiration for coloring designs
from its architecture, art and culture.

The floor mosaics in Venice's most beautiful buildings
provided some of the best designs for coloring pages,
perhaps even more so than Parisian flooring did when I was
researching the Love Paris Adult Coloring book.

The coloring pages in this book are on one side so you
can cut out your work if you wish. Some of the pages
have titles, (so you know which bit of Venice you are
coloring in,) but you can cut around these too.

The pages are suitable for colored pencil, crayon and water
based ink. If you want to use anything heavier, I
recommend placing a piece of card under the
page and using this page as a test page.

Louisa

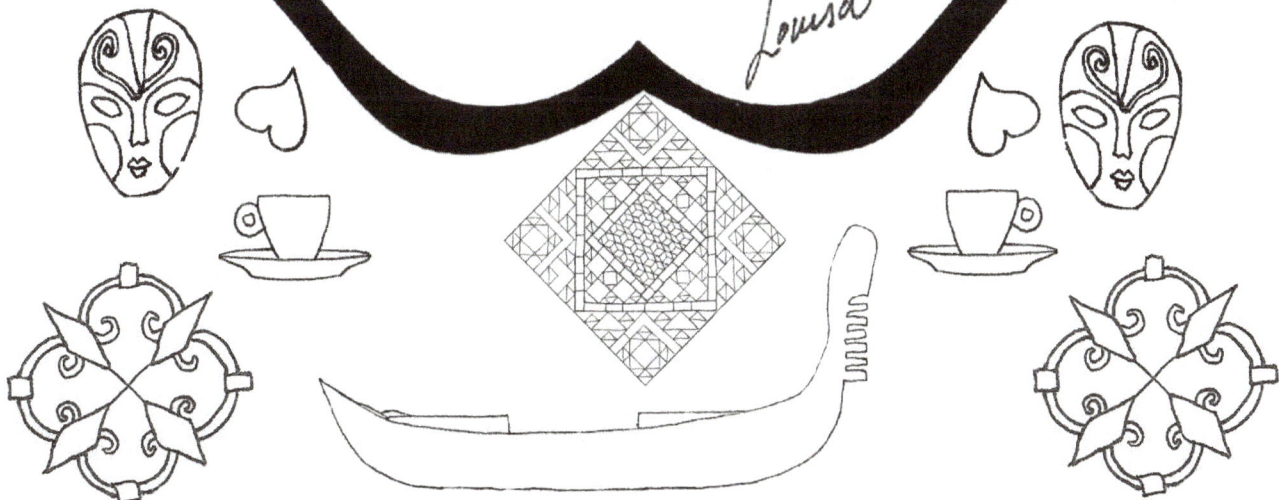

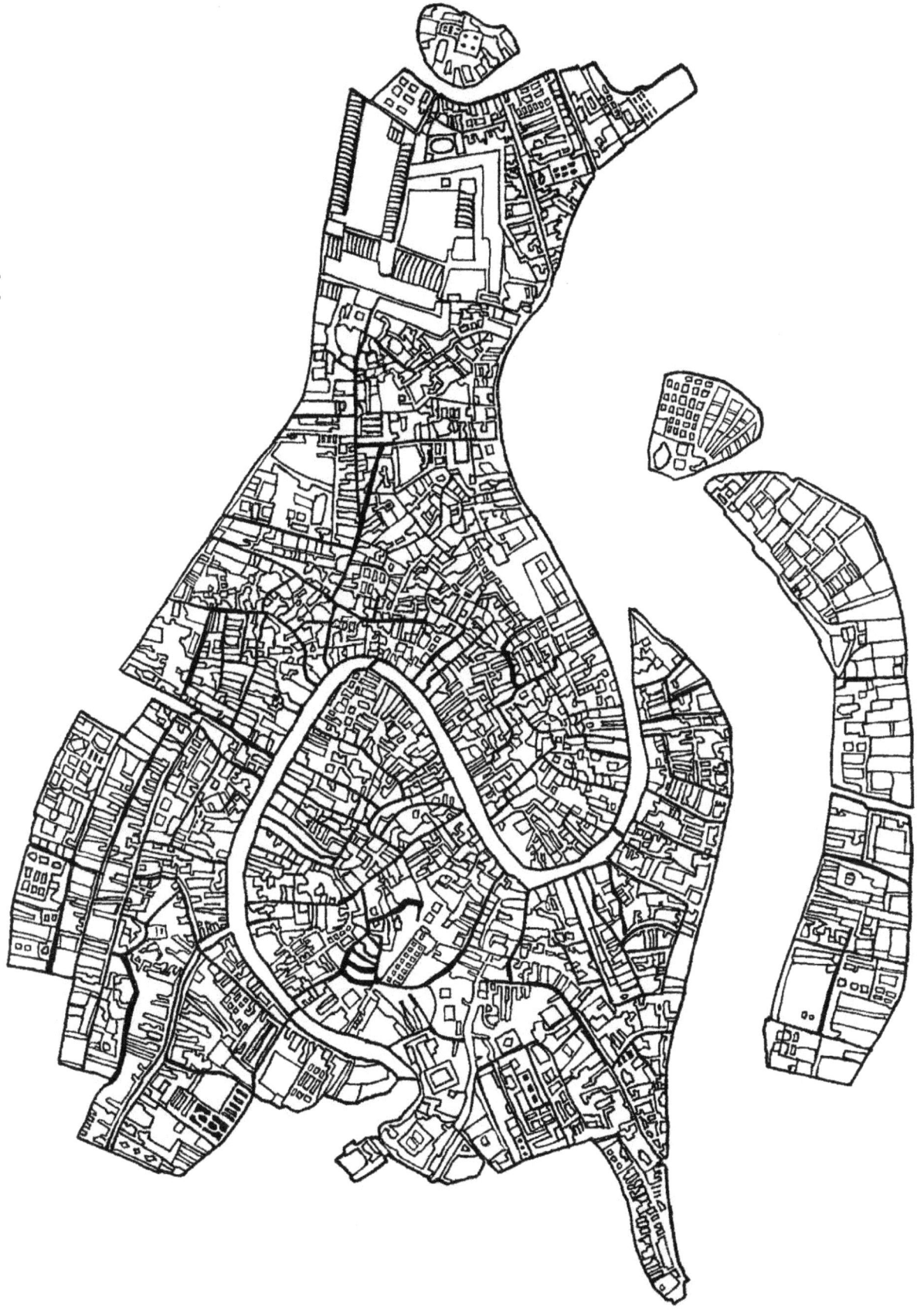

Mappa di Venezia

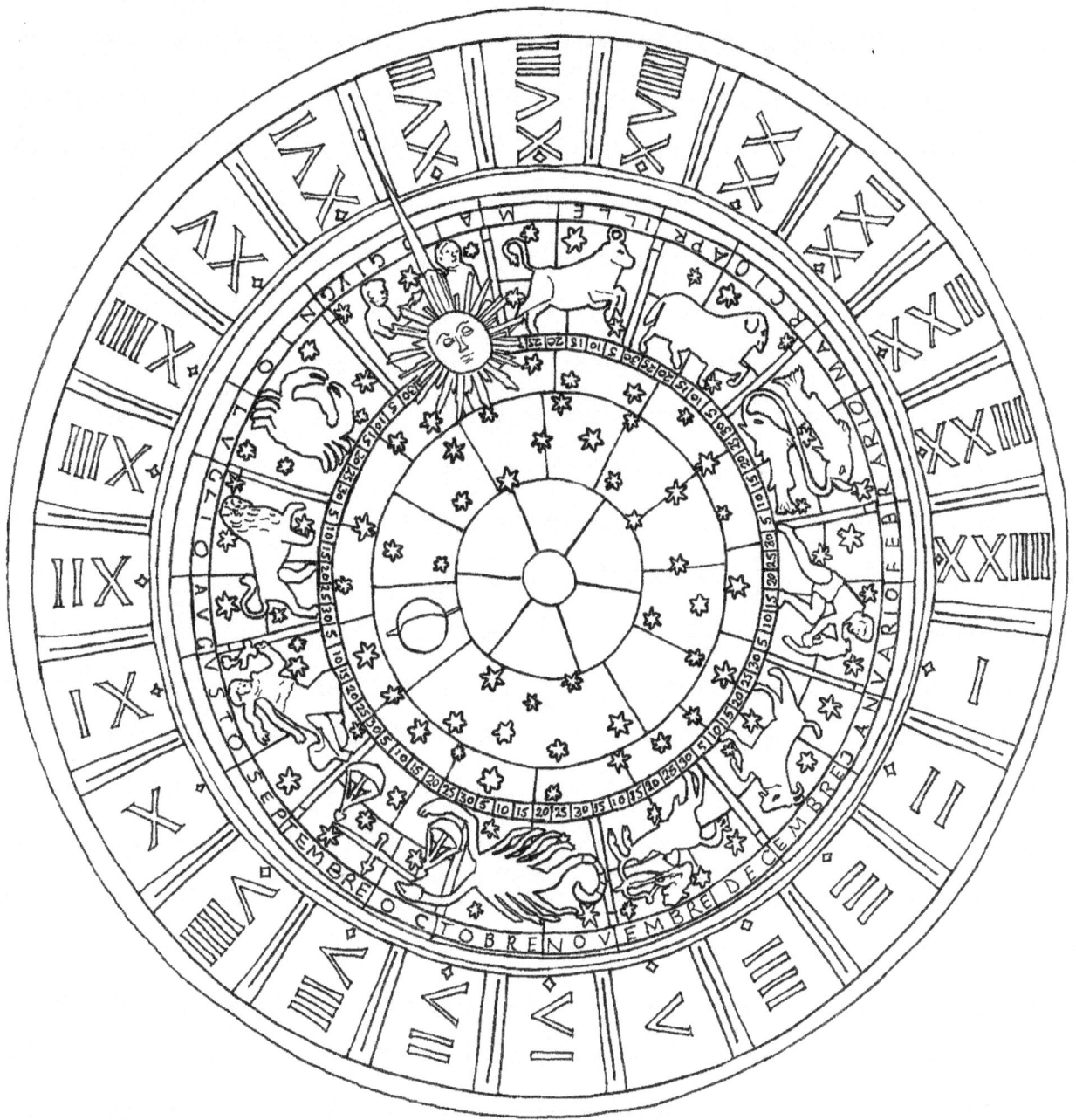

TORRE DELL'OROLOGIO

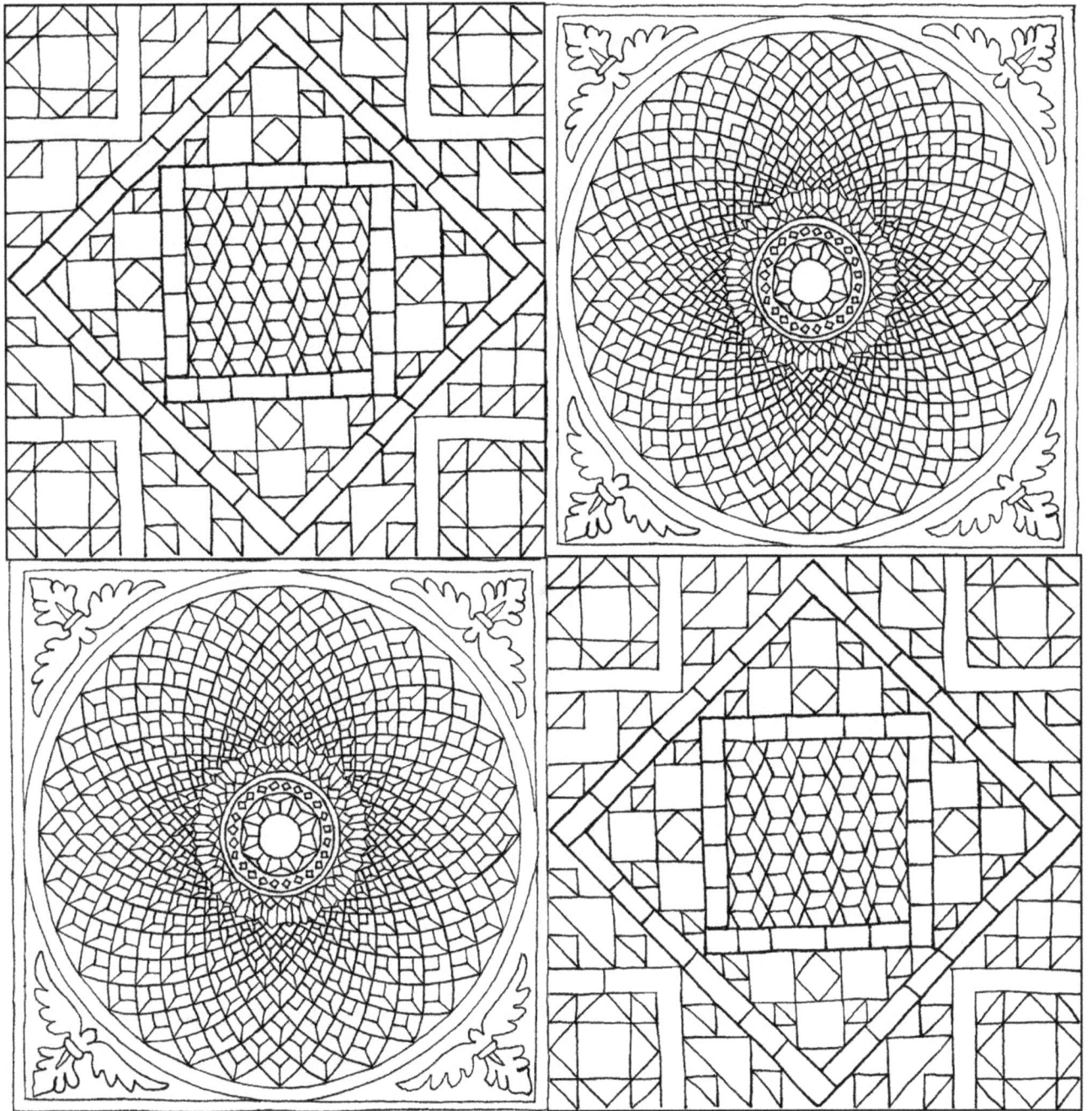

SAINT MARK'S BASILICA

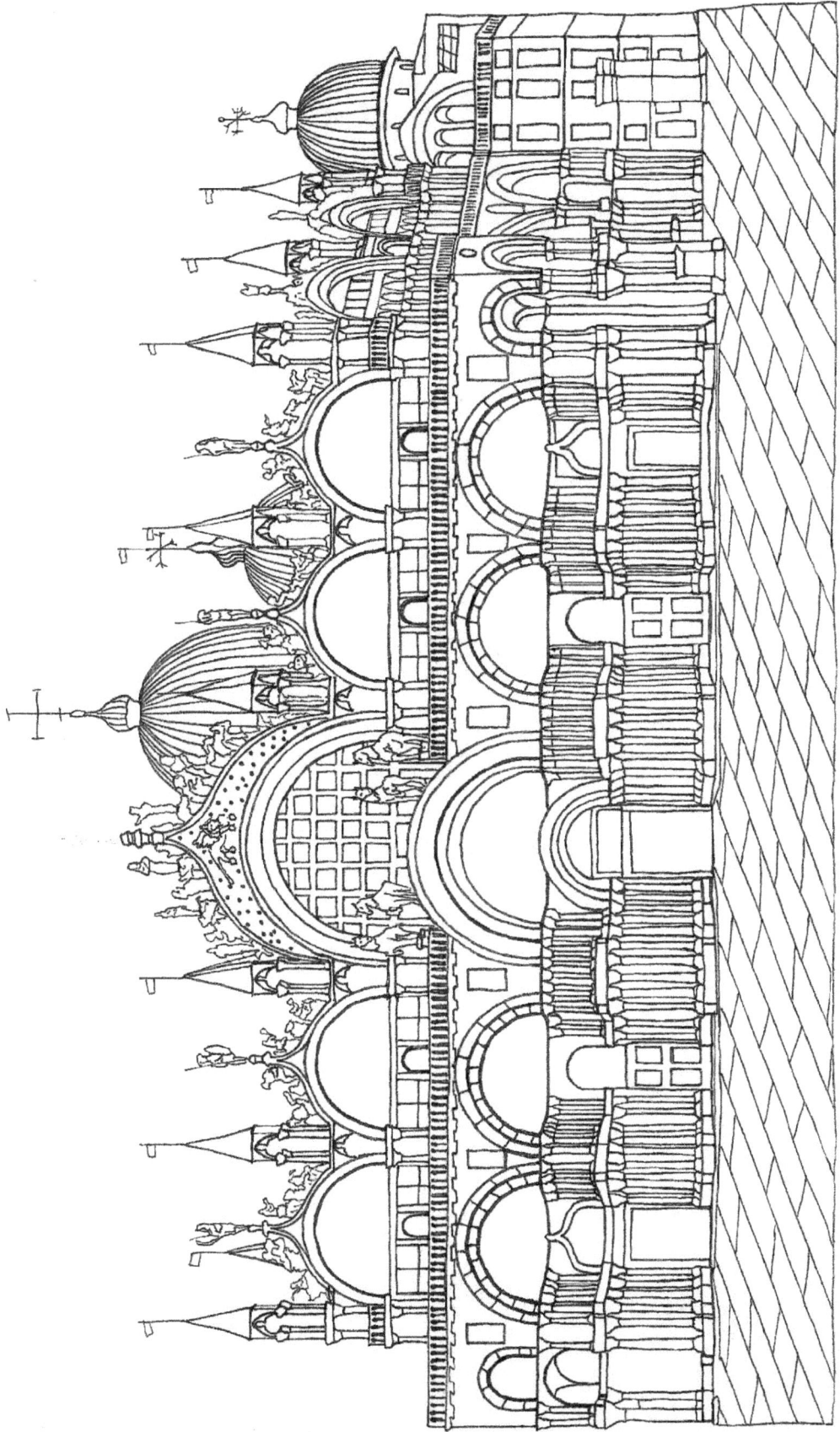

Basilica di San Marco

FLORIAN

CAFE

FLORIAN

TEA-ROOM

FLORIAN

BAR

Carnevale di Venezia

PALA D'ORO

Santa Maria della Salute

PAVLO BARBO M ANT MAVROCE NO

LEONARDO LAV E N VENET DVC

ALEXANDRI LIOPARDI OPVS ANNO

PONTE DI DI RIALTO CANAL GRANDE

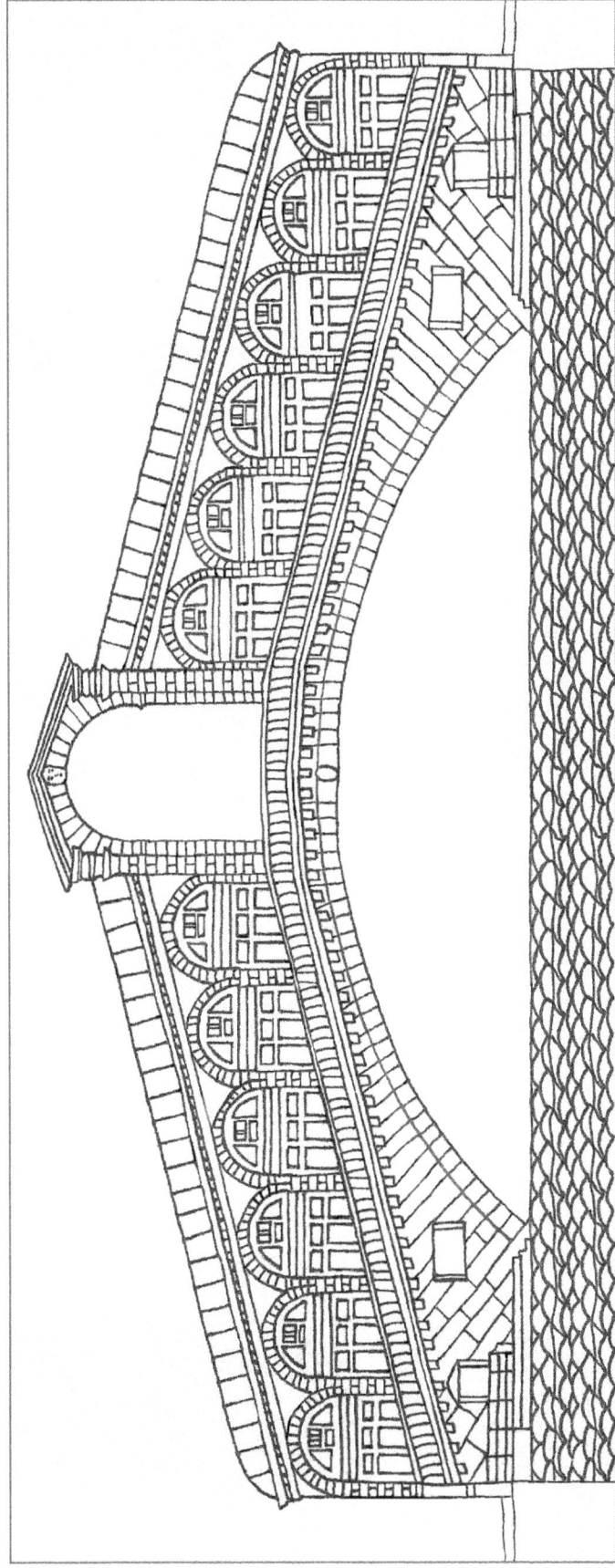

The Chinese Room, Caffè Florian

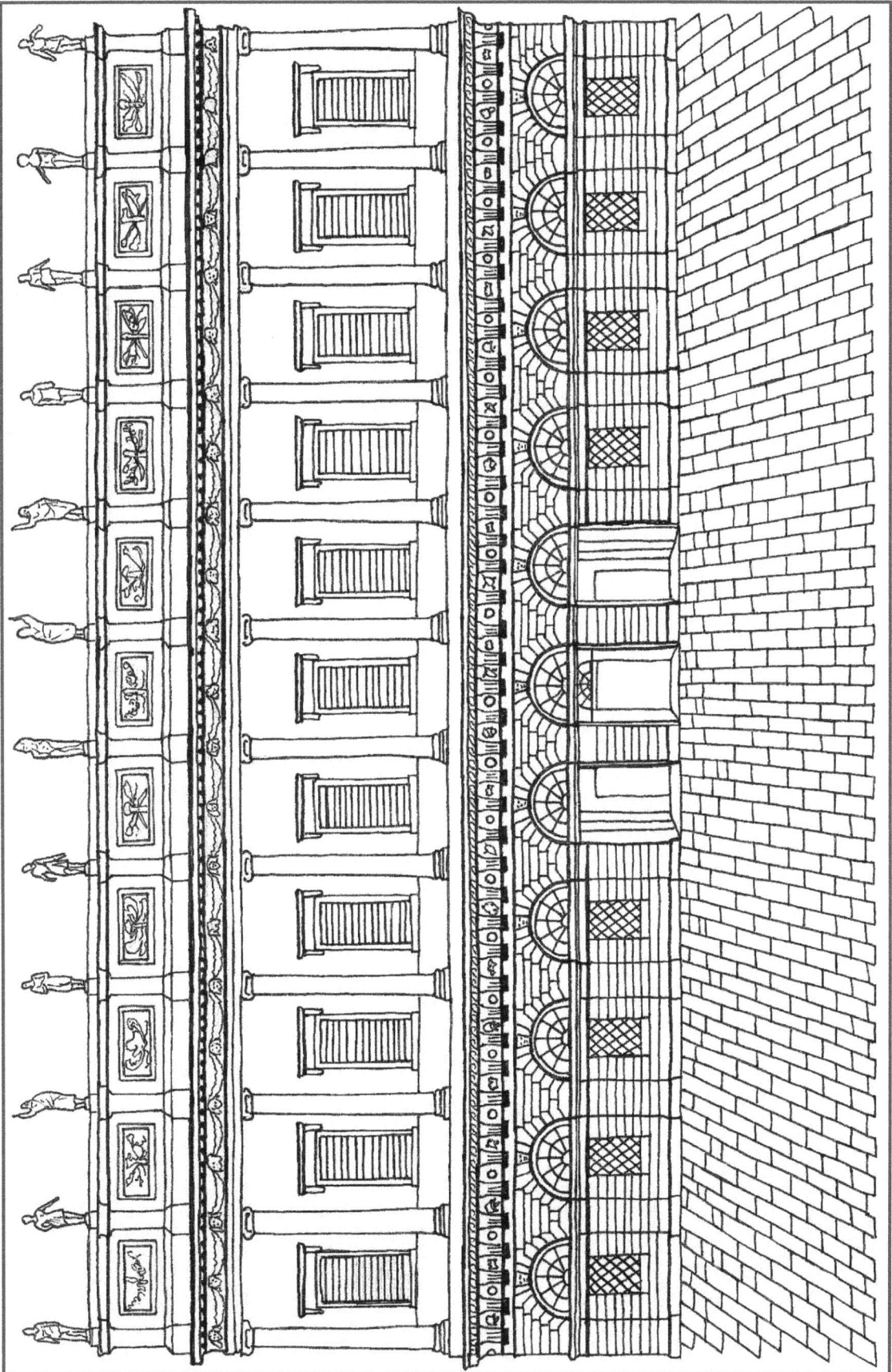

Alliance Française di Venezia

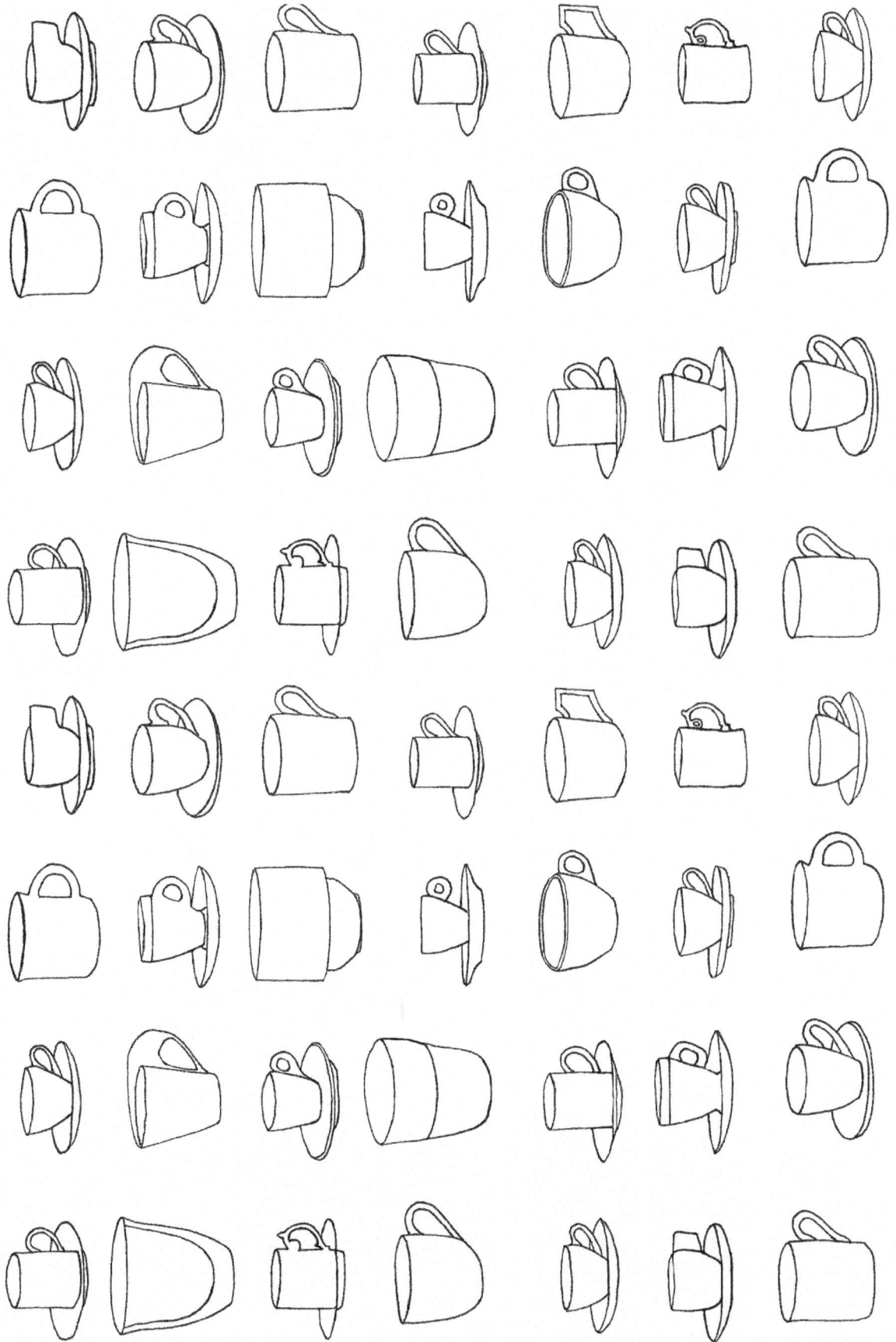

www.ingramcontent.com/pod-product-compliance
Lightning Source LLC
Chambersburg PA
CBHW081227020426
42331CB00012B/3097